D0475269

JUL   2005

TIN

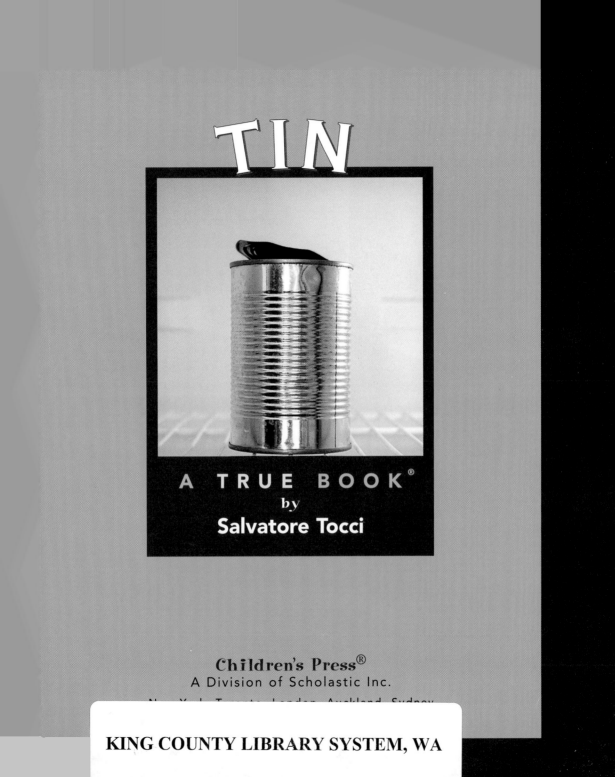

A TRUE BOOK®

by

Salvatore Tocci

Children's Press®
A Division of Scholastic Inc.

New York   Toronto   London   Auckland   Sydney

Tin solder is used to hold together the approximately five hundred pieces of metal that make up a saxophone.

Reading Consultant
Julia McKenzie Munemo, MEd
New York, New York

Science Consultant
John A. Benner
Austin, Texas

The photo on the cover shows tin cans ready for recycling. The photo on the title page shows an open tin can in a refrigerator.

The author and the publisher are not responsible for injuries or accidents that occur during or from any experiments. Experiments should be conducted in the presence of or with the help of an adult. Any instructions of the experiments that require the use of sharp, hot, or other unsafe items should be conducted by or with the help of an adult.

Library of Congress Cataloging-in-Publication Data

Tocci, Salvatore.
    Tin / by Salvatore Tocci.
      p. cm. — (A true book)
Includes bibliographical references and index.
    ISBN 0-516-23697-0 (lib. bdg.)   0-516-25573-8 (pbk.)
      1. Tin—Juvenile literature.   I. Title. II. Series.
QD181.S7T57 2005
546'.686—dc22   2004013144

Contents

When was the last time you heard someone play an organ?

What's Your Favorite Musical Instrument?

Do you play a musical instrument? Perhaps you take clarinet lessons or piano lessons. Even if you don't play an instrument, you may like to listen to a certain one. Some people like to listen to an organ. The most likely place to hear someone playing an organ is in a church.

During the 1800s, people in northern Europe began to notice something strange happening to their church organs. The solid pipes where the sounds came out were turning into a grayish powder. People noticed that some of the pipes would crumble into powder, or corrode, when the temperature inside the church dropped, especially during long, cold winters.

People were not sure why these pipes were turning into a grayish powder. Some suggested it was the work of the devil. Others believed that some kind of strange disease was affecting the metal pipes. They began to

Whenever it got cold outside, the organ pipes inside the churches would start to crumble into powder.

refer to this problem as "tin disease" because the organ pipes were made from tin.

Scientists later discovered why these pipes were turning into powder. It had to do with the tin that was used to make them. Unlike other metals, tin does something very unusual in cold weather.

Why Is Tin So Unusual?

Tin is an element. An **element** is the building block of matter. **Matter** is the stuff or material that makes up everything in the universe. This book, the chair you are sitting on, and even you are made of matter.

There are millions of different kinds of matter. However,

there are just a few more than one hundred different elements. How can so many different kinds of matter be made up of so few elements? Think about the English language. Just twenty-six letters can be arranged to make up all the words in the English language. Likewise, the one hundred or so elements can be arranged to make up all the kinds of matter in the universe.

Every element has both a name and a symbol made up of one, two, or three letters. The symbol for tin is Sn. This symbol comes from the Latin word *stannum*, which was used by the ancient Romans to mean "tin."

Tin, like most other elements, is a metal. All metals are **conductors**, which allow electricity to pass through them. Tin is also **ductile**, which means it can be drawn

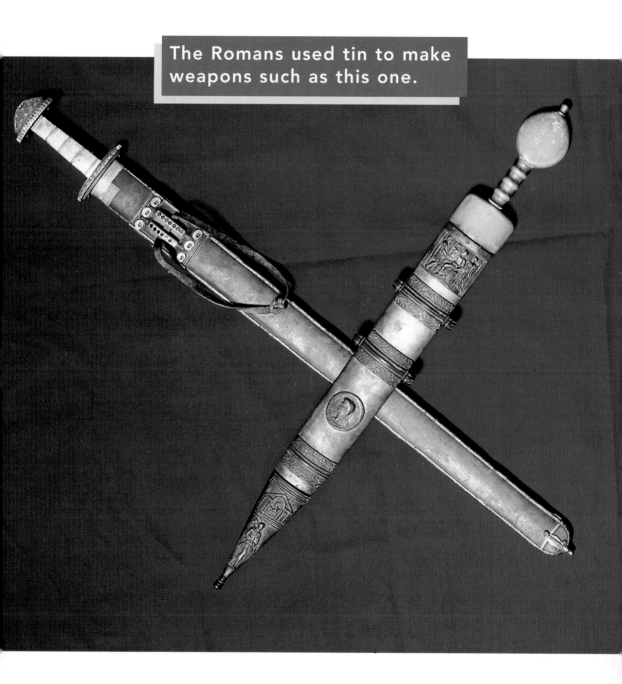

The Romans used tin to make weapons such as this one.

out into a wire or pounded thin. Tin is **malleable**, which means it can be hammered or twisted into different shapes without breaking.

A thin layer of tin coats the steel that is used to make cans for storing food. Steel rusts when it is moist and exposed to the air. Tin, how-ever, does not rust. The thin layer of tin prevents rust from forming inside the can and spoiling the food.

Foods are stored in cans made of steel covered with a thin layer of tin to prevent rust.

Testing Cans

See how simple it is to find out if a can is made from aluminum or from steel and tin. All you need is a magnet. Aluminum is not magnetic. Steel, however, is magnetic. If the can is attracted to the magnet, it contains steel that has been coated with a thin layer of tin. What kinds of foods are stored in cans that contain tin?

Although it is ductile, malleable, and conducts electricity, tin does something very unusual that makes it different from most metals. In fact, tin is so different that under certain conditions, it isn't even considered a metal. At room temperature, tin is a silvery-white metal that conducts electricity. When the temperature drops below 55 degrees Fahrenheit (13 degrees Celsius), tin slowly turns into a grayish powder. Cold weather caused the organ pipes in northern Europe to turn into powder. Although this powder is still tin, it is no longer a metal because the powder does not conduct electricity.

Scientists discovered that mixing tin with one or more other elements prevents tin from turning into a powder in cold temperatures. This mixing of tin and other elements produces an **alloy**. Today, organ pipes are made

No matter how cold it gets, these organ pipes will never corrode because they are made of a tin alloy.

from a tin alloy that will not corrode in cold temperatures. Tin alloys are used for more than just making organ pipes.

How Are Tin Alloys Used?

One of the most common uses of tin alloys is in making **solder**, which is an alloy made of tin and iron. Iron is another metallic element. Solder is used to join metal parts. The solder is placed on the metal parts that are

Tin makes up approximately 70 percent of the solder used to make metal connections in electronic devices, such as computers and televisions.

to be joined. The solder is heated to its melting point and then allowed to cool. As the solder turns back into a solid, it forms a strong bond between the metal parts. Tin has a low melting point compared with most other metals. This allows the heat to melt only the solder, not the metal parts that are to be joined.

Bronze is another tin alloy, which is made by mixing tin

and copper. This alloy was first made almost five thousand years ago, which was the start of a time known as the Bronze Age. Before then, people used stones to make tools and weapons. These stone items were difficult to make and wore out from repeated use.

Although copper was available before the Bronze Age, it is too soft to be useful for making tools and weapons.

The Bronze Age started when people discovered that copper could be made much harder by mixing it with tin. The two metals were melted by heating them together in a small furnace. The alloy was then poured into a stone mold. After cooling, the bronze object was removed from the mold. The final step involved using a copper or stone tool to finish the object.

These objects were made from bronze more than four thousand years ago.

The bronze weapons
that were made included
arrowheads and daggers.

The bronze tools included hammers, axes, and sickles for harvesting crops. These bronze objects were much stronger and lasted longer than the earlier stone tools. Hunters could spend more time catching animals and less time making the tools they needed. Farmers could also grow more crops and cultivate more land with these improved tools.

Today, bronze is used to make buttons, statues, and medals, such as those given to athletes who finish third in Olympic games. Among the largest objects made from bronze are bells. The bronze used to make bells is about 80 percent copper and 20 percent tin. This alloy contains just the right combination to produce a clear, rich tone when a bronze bell is struck.

Bronze does not rust or corrode easily. However, bronze does weather over time. The copper in the alloy develops a thin, green coating known as a patina. After a patina has formed, the bronze will slowly start to rust. This process is so slow that a bronze bell will last for hundreds of years.

Pewter is another tin alloy. Besides tin, pewter contains the element copper, which is

The pewter used to make these candlesticks contains more than 90 percent tin.

added for strength. Pewter is used to make candlesticks, figurines, and jewelry. The use of pewter to make jewelry can be traced back more than two thousand years to Egypt and China. Later, the ancient Romans used pewter to make dishes, eating utensils, and official seals.

Tin alloys play an important role in car manufacturing. A tin-lead alloy keeps metal parts moving smoothly in

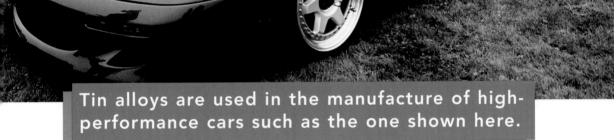

Tin alloys are used in the manufacture of high-performance cars such as the one shown here.

engines. A tin-zinc alloy is used on brake parts so that they do not corrode. A tin-aluminum alloy is used to make parts for high-performance engines.

How Are Tin Compounds Used?

Tin alloys are examples of **mixtures** in which two or more elements are mixed, but retain their individual properties. Tin is used not only to make alloys but also to make **compounds**. A compound is different from

The shiny surface of this marble top was produced by polishing it with a tin compound.

a mixture. A compound consists of two or more elements that are joined together. Tin compounds have a variety of uses.

Seeing the Difference

Here's a simple way to see the difference between a mixture and a compound. Mix some miniature and regular-size marshmallows in a bowl. Cut several holes in the bottom of an empty shoe box. The holes should be large enough to allow only the miniature marshmallows to pass through. Dump the marshmallows from the bowl into the shoe box. Gently shake the box.

Notice how easy it is to separate the two different-size marshmallows. How else might you separate them? Now use toothpicks to join two different-size marshmallows. Can you separate these by shaking them in the shoe box? Which marshmallows represent a mixture? Which ones represent a compound?

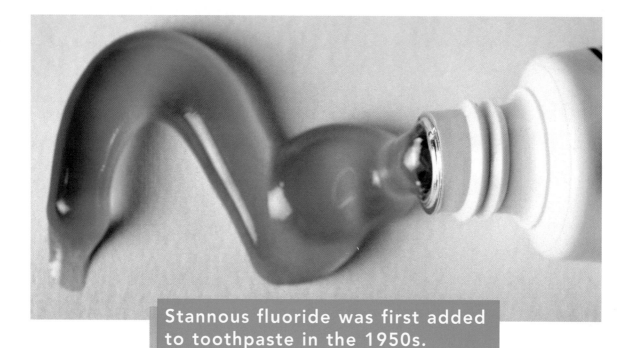
Stannous fluoride was first added to toothpaste in the 1950s.

If you look at the label on a toothpaste tube, you might see the words *stannous fluoride*. *Stannous* comes from the Latin word for tin, *stannum*. Stannous fluoride is the name of a compound that contains tin. The other element in this compound is fluorine. Stannous fluoride is added to toothpaste to help prevent tooth decay. Tin chloride is a compound used to make dyes, plastics, and glass. Tin oxide is a compound used to polish steel, marble, and glass.

The largest single use of a tin compound is in making a material called polyvinyl chloride (PVC). Most PVC is

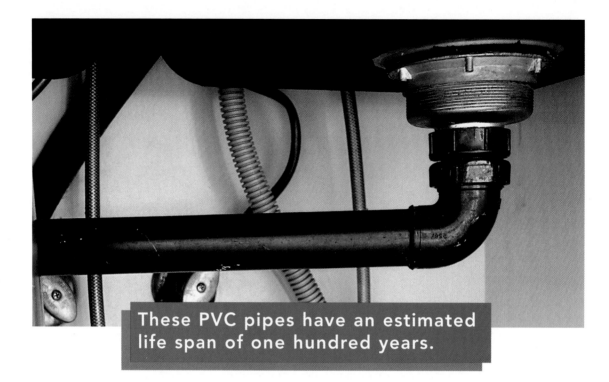

These PVC pipes have an estimated life span of one hundred years.

used in construction, mainly in pipes used for plumbing and irrigation systems. PVC has several useful properties. It can bend without breaking. It will never rust, pit, or corrode. However, PVC cannot tolerate the high temperatures that are needed to make it. A tin compound is added to prevent the PVC from breaking down during the manufacturing process.

Tin alloys and tin compounds may not break down, even in cold weather. However, as an element, tin is not as stable. You read that organ pipes made of tin corroded in cold weather. "Tin disease" is also thought to have affected other events in history.

In 1910, Robert Scott, a British explorer, set out with an expedition to become the first humans to reach the South Pole. Scott and his men reached the pole, but they were not the first.

Tragedy struck when Scott and his men died on their return trip. Some people say one reason for the explorers' deaths was the tin solder used to make the cans for storing the kerosene fuel. The tin corroded because of the cold, allowing the

kerosene to leak. As a result, Scott and his group of men had no fuel to burn to keep warm or to heat their meals.

Fun Facts About Tin

- Tin solder is used to hold together the approximately five hundred pieces of metal that make up a saxophone.

- An alloy containing tin is used for dental fillings. The other two metals in this alloy are silver and copper.

- A tin alloy was used to build one of the world's most powerful magnets, which weighs about 7 tons.

- Tin is a scarce element that makes up only two parts per million of Earth's crust.

- When tin is bent rapidly, it makes a strange squealing noise called a "tin cry."

- Almost one-third of the tin used in the United States comes from recycling, mainly of tin-coated steel cans.

- The World Peace Bell, the largest free-swinging bronze bell in the world, is located in Newport, Kentucky. The bell weighs 33 tons.

To Find Out More

To find out more about tin, check out these additional resources.

Books

Abraham, Fern-Rae. **Tin Craft: A Workbook.** Sunstone Press, 1994.

Kitahara, Teruhisa. **1000 Tin Toys.** Taschen, 2002.

Organizations and Online Sites

Tin

http://www.ancientroute
.com/resource/metal/tin.htm

Learn more about the
sources and history of tin.
This site also provides
information about refer-
ences made to tin in
the Bible.

Washington State Department of Ecology

http://www.ecy.wa.gov/
programs/swfa/kidspage/
tin.html

Read about the recycling of
tin cans. Find out what
"detinning" involves and
how this process is used to
recover scrap metal to
make new cans.

American Bronze Foundry

http://www.americanbronze
.com/whatsbronze.htm

Trace the history of the
making of bronze, starting
with the ancient Sumerians
in the Tigris-Euphrates
River Valley around 3500 B.C.
Read how bronze was used
to make guns in Europe
during the fourteenth,
fifteenth, and sixteenth
centuries.

Tin

http://pearl1.lanl.gov/
periodic/elements/50.html

This site has information
about the sources, properties, and forms of tin. Find
out how tin is used in the
making of window glass.

Important Words

alloy substance made by mixing a metal with one or more other elements

compound substance formed when two or more elements are joined

conductor substance through which electricity or heat passes

ductile capable of being drawn into a wire or pressed thin

element building block of matter

malleable capable of being hammered or twisted into different shapes without breaking

matter stuff or material that makes up everything in the universe

mixture substance made when two or more elements are combined but retain their individual properties

solder alloy that contains tin and is used to join metal parts

Index

Meet the Author

Salvatore Tocci is a science writer who lives in East Hampton, New York with his wife Patti. He was a high school biology and chemistry teacher for almost thirty years. His books include a high school chemistry textbook and an elementary school series that encourages students to perform experiments to learn about science. He uses tin solder to join metal parts, such as rail joints, on his HO train layout.